YOU M

THIS

1967

MILESTONES, MEMORIES,
TRIVIA AND FACTS, NEWS EVENTS,
PROMINENT PERSONALITIES &
SPORTS HIGHLIGHTS OF THE YEAR

TO: *Lisa Beth*

FROM: *Mom*

MESSAGE: *Wow! Am I getting old!!*

*selected and researched
by
mary a. pradt*

WARNER **W** TREASURES™

PUBLISHED BY WARNER BOOKS

A TIME WARNER COMPANY

Warner Books, Inc.
1271 Avenue of the Americas
New York, New York 10020

Warner Treasures is a
trademark of Warner Books, Inc.

Ⓦ A Time Warner Company
DESIGN:
CAROL BOKUNIEWICZ DESIGN
PRINTED IN SINGAPORE
FIRST PRINTING : MAY 1995
10 9 8 7 6 5 4 3 2 1
ISBN : 0-446-91044-9

Sobering casualties were reported on the war front.

Increasing numbers of Americans were dying in Vietnam, mostly from mines or booby traps, one trademark of guerrilla warfare. General William Westmoreland called for more troops in Vietnam.

muhammad ali's draft-exemption
tion case was a cause célèbre. Ali had been reclassified 1-A but refused to serve for religious reasons. He was sentenced to 5 years in jail, fined $10,000, and the World Boxing Association stripped him of his world heavyweight title.

THREE ASTRONAUTS, **VIRGIL I. GRISSOM, EDWARD H. WHITE, AND ROGER B. CHAFFEE,** WERE KILLED ON JANUARY 27, ON THE GROUND AT LAUNCHING PAD 34 AT CAPE KENNEDY, AT THE BEGINNING OF A FULL-SCALE SIMULATION OF THE EARTH-ORBITING FLIGHT THEY WOULD HAVE ATTEMPTED IN FEBRUARY. THEY WERE THE FIRST AMERICAN CASUALTIES OF THE SPACE RACE. THE *SURVEYOR* SPACECRAFT REACHED THE MOON AND GATHERED DATA AND PHO-TOGRAPHS. ALL WAS IN PREPARATION FOR THE MANNED MOON SHOOT.

IN MARCH 10,000 HIPPIES GATHERED IN CENTRAL PARK FOR A **BE-IN.** THE OVER-30 SET WENT TO THE FIFTH AVENUE EASTER DAY PARADE INSTEAD.

a washington march on the Pentagon against the war in October became aggressive. About 250 people were arrested, including Norman Mailer and Dave Dellinger of the National Mobilization Committee to End the War.

The Supreme Court extended First Amendment rights, overturning a judgment against *Life* magazine for invasion of privacy. Any falsehoods must be proved to be deliberate or reckless. This case extended the landmark libel decision **N.Y. Times vs. Sullivan** of 1964.

newsreel

THURGOOD MARSHALL, FORMER SOLICITOR GENERAL AND PREVIOUSLY SUCCESSFUL LITIGATOR FOR THE NAACP, IN AUGUST BECAME THE FIRST BLACK NAMED TO THE U.S. SUPREME COURT.

RACE RIOTS swept the country in the summer of 1967. Otto Kerner was appointed head of a commission to investigate causes. In July there was rioting in Detroit in which 31 died. The mayor said his city looked like Berlin after WWII. In New York, Puerto Rican youths rioted, looted, and burned cars. There were riots in Toledo, Grand Rapids, and elsewhere. Stokely Carmichael called for Black revolution. Politically aware whites and Blacks used the word "BLACK" instead of the previously more acceptable term "NEGRO."

CANADA'S EXPO '67 WAS ONE OF THE MOST SUCCESSFUL WORLD'S FAIRS IN HISTORY.

Expo '67 Habitat

THE SUPERTANKER *TORREY CANYON* WAS WRECKED OFF THE FRENCH COAST, CAUSING A GIGANTIC OIL SPILL.

international

headlines

Stalin's daughter, **svetlana alliluyeva,** defected to the West, with CIA help, at a rather embarrassing time, as LBJ was trying to pursue "peaceful engagement" with the USSR.

Israel defeated Arab forces in a six-day war in June and occupied the Sinai Peninsula and other key territories, most of which were relinquished over the next three decades.

CHINA WAS IN UPHEAVAL, WITH BATTLES AMONG FACTIONS, TORTURE OF EACH OTHER'S PRISONERS, AND GROWING OPPOSITION TO MAO'S CULTURAL REVOLUTION.

LBJ VISITED THE TROOPS IN VIETNAM FOR CHRISTMAS.

BIAFRA, the Eastern region of Nigeria, seceded. The ensuing civil war involved religious and tribal differences (Muslims/Hausa vs. animist and Christian Ibo people). The Biafran war would become a tragedy of starving children and wandering, homeless people.

The Soviets had a huge celebration, marked by an arms show featuring 5 new missiles, one of them 110 feet long. The occasion was **the 50th anniversary of the Russian Revolution.**

5

The Monterey Pop Festival drew 50,000 people. It was a sea of long hair, flowers, good vibes, and great dope. Artists included the Byrds, Otis Redding, the Mamas and the Papas, Jefferson Airplane, and Indian sitarist Ravi Shankar. New talents at the fest were Janis Joplin's Big Brother and the Holding Company, the Who, and a beautiful, young **jimi hendrix.**

Politics and pop were inter-twined. **JOAN BAEZ** sang for reporters and then was arrested at an induction center demonstration in Oakland, CA, in October.

AMERICA CONSUMED 12 BILLION CANS OF BEER AND 5.3 BILLION CANS OF SOFT DRINKS DURING THE YEAR.

the concorde,

the world's first supersonic aircraft, was unveiled in Toulouse, France. It was a joint British–French venture.

DR. CHRISTIAAN BARNARD OF SOUTH AFRICA PERFORMED THE FIRST HEART TRANSPLANT. THE PATIENT LIVED 18 DAYS.

cultural

milestones

The first microwave oven was introduced.

Make the greatest cooking discovery since fire.

Radarange made only by Amana.

THE NATIONAL ORGANIZATION FOR WOMEN ADOPTED A BILL OF RIGHTS FOR WOMEN.

THE FIRST SCHOOL FOR UNMARRIED PREGNANT TEENAGED GIRLS OPENED IN NEW YORK ON JUNE 23, 1967.

THE POPULATION OF THE U.S. REACHED 200 MILLION. PROJECTED DATE FOR A POPULATION OF 500 MILLION, BARRING CATASTROPHE, WAS THE YEAR 2015.

top-rated tv shows of the 1967 season:

1. "The Andy Griffith Show" (CBS) **6.** "Bonanza" (NBC)

2. "The Lucy Show" (CBS) **7.** "The Red Skelton Show" (CBS)

3. "Gomer Pyle, U.S.M.C." (CBS) **8.** "The Dean Martin Show" (NBC)

4. "Gunsmoke" (CBS) **9.** "The Jackie Gleason Show" (CBS)

5. "Family Affair" (CBS) **10.** "Saturday Night at the Movies" (NBC)

Ranking just under the Top 10 were :
"BEWITCHED" (ABC) "THE BEVERLY HILLBILLIES" (CBS)
"THE ED SULLIVAN SHOW" (CBS) "THE VIRGINIAN" (NBC)
"THE FRIDAY NIGHT MOVIE" (CBS) "GREEN ACRES" (CBS)
"THE LAWRENCE WELK SHOW" (ABC)
"THE SMOTHERS BROTHERS COMEDY HOUR" (CBS)
"GENTLE BEN" (CBS)
"TUESDAY NIGHT AT THE MOVIES" (NBC)

Premieres in September 1967—Sally Field as
"The Flying Nun," "The Carol Burnett
Show," "Ironside," and "Mannix."

A TV audience of 51,180,000 tuned in to the first Super Bowl broadcast on January 15, 1967.

There were 55,130,000 TV households in America, 93.6% of homes. Color TVs were being bought in greater numbers, but sales didn't really take off until the seventies; in 1966 less than 10 percent of TV households had color sets. Average amount of time spent watching TV was 5 hours 42 minutes a day, up 10 minutes from 1966. Daily viewing would be over 6 hours a day in 1972.

"the fugitive"

stopped running. On August 29, 1967, Dr. Richard Kimble found the one-armed man. The final episode was watched by 72 percent of America's TV viewers.

Elvis & Priscilla!

On May 1, 1967, **ELVIS PRESLEY,** 32, married his longtime girlfriend, **PRISCILLA BEAULIEU,** 21. Priscilla was radiant in a white chiffon dress embroidered with tiny pearls and complemented by a full chiffon veil. The nuptials, in Las Vegas, were attended by 14 close friends. A champagne breakfast for 100 followed. The couple met in 1959 when the groom was serving with the U.S. Army in Germany, and she, the daughter of an air force officer, was attending high school in Frankfurt. Both were originally from Memphis. The Presleys would later become the parents of **LISA MARIE,** who grew up to marry singer **MICHAEL JACKSON** in 1994.

celeb wedding of the year

milestones

DEATHS

Bruce Barton,
adman and author of the best-selling biography of Jesus, *The Man Nobody Knows*, died at 80.

Primo Carnera,
boxer, model for *The Harder They Fall*, died at 60.

John Coltrane,
tenor sax great, died at 40.

Bernard Fall,
French authority on Vietnam, was killed there, at 40, while on patrol with U.S. marines.

Geraldine Farrar,
great prima donna of the Met, died at 85.

Jimmy Foxx,
Baseball Hall of Famer, died at 59.

John Nance Garner,
VP for two terms under FDR, died at 98.

Woody Guthrie,
folksinger and composer, died at 55.

Edward Hopper,
American painter, died at 84.

Vivien Leigh,
who won Oscars as Scarlett O'Hara in *Gone With the Wind* and as Blanche du Bois in *A Streetcar Named Desire*, died at 53.

Henry Luce,
founder of *Time*, *Life*, and *Fortune*, died at 68.

Jayne Mansfield,
blonde bombshell sex symbol, was killed in a car crash at 34.

births

JULIA ROBERTS, actress and star of such smash movies as *Pretty Woman* and *The Pelican Brief*, was born on October 28.

LISA BONET, actress best known for her role on *The Cosby Show*, was born on November 16.

AMY CARTER, daughter of President Jimmy Carter, was born on October 19.

BORIS BECKER, German tennis star, was born on November 22.

JIM ABBOTT, All-Star one-armed pitcher for the New York Yankees, was born on September 19.

Jayne Mansfield

11

'67

hit music

1. **to sir with love** Lulu (from the movie *To Sir With Love*)
2. **daydream believer** Monkees
3. **windy** Association
4. **ode to billie joe** Bobby Gentry
5. **groovin'** Young Rascals
6. **somethin' stupid** Nancy and Frank Sinatra
7. **the letter** Box Tops

It was arguably one of the greatest years in rock history, although this was not necessarily reflected by the top-charted singles.

8. **light my fire** The Doors
9. **happy together** Turtles
10. **hello goodbye** Beatles
11. **respect** Aretha Franklin
12. **kind of a drag** Buckinghams
13. **incense and peppermints** Strawberry Alarm Clock
14. **love is here and now you've gone** Supremes
15. **ruby tuesday** Rolling Stones
16. **all you need is love** Beatles
17. **the happening** Supremes
18. **penny lane** Beatles

All these sides reached #1 on the charts.

Lulu

ALSO ON THE CHART:

"SOUL MAN," SAM AND DAVE;

"GEORGY GIRL" SEEKERS;

"DON'T SLEEP IN THE SUBWAY" PETULA CLARK

"A NATURAL WOMAN" ARETHA FRANKLIN

"I HEARD IT THROUGH THE GRAPEVINE" GLADYS KNIGHT AND THE PIPS

"WHITE RABBIT" JEFFERSON AIRPLANE

"STRAWBERRY FIELDS FOREVER" BEATLES

"SUNDAY WILL NEVER BE THE SAME" SPANKY AND OUR GANG

"DANDELION" ROLLING STONES

bestselling

fiction

1. **the arrangement**
elia kazan

2. **the confessions of nat turner**
william styron, tied with

3. **the chosen**
chaim potok

4. **topaz**
leon uris

5. **christy**
catherine marshall

6. **the eighth day**
thornton wilder

7. **rosemary's baby**
ira levin

8. **the plot**
irving wallace

9. **the gabriel hounds**
mary stewart

10. **the exhibitionist**
henry sutton

Although the country was torn by riots, antiwar sentiment, and student revolt, the bestseller lists didn't really reflect this.

14

Important books of the year included **LA VIDA,** a prizewinning documentary account of Puerto Rican life on the island and in New York by **OSCAR LEWIS;** *THE MEDIUM IS THE MESSAGE* by **MARSHALL MCLUHAN** and **QUENTIN FIORE;** *A GARDEN OF EARTHLY DELIGHTS,* by **JOYCE CAROL OATES;** and *THE MAN WHO CRIED I AM,* by **JOHN A. WILLIAMS.**

books

15

mickey mantle hit his

500th career home run at Yankee Stadium May 14, becoming the 6th player to reach that record.

Mickey Mantle

BILLIE JEAN KING SWEPT THE WOMEN'S SINGLES AT WIMBLEDON.

16

The America's Cup was successfully defended by the U.S. yacht *Intrepid*, defeating the Australian challenger *Dame Pattie*.

the first super bowl was won

January 15 by the Green Bay Packers, who defeated the Kansas City Chiefs, 35–10. Green Bay had won the NFL championship over the Dallas Cowboys, while the Chiefs had beat the Buffalo Bills in the AFL championship.

At the end of 1967, the Packers beat the Dallas Cowboys with a touchdown scored from the one-yard line by Bart Starr, with 13 seconds left in the game. In the AFL championship game, the Oakland Raiders destroyed the Houston Oilers, 40–7. The Pack would go on to win Super Bowl II in January 1968, and legendary coach **VINCE LOMBARDI** would retire.

sports

PEGGY FLEMING

triumphed at US figure skating championships. She fell during her freestyle event at the world championships but went on to win the women's singles title for the 2nd year running.

COLLEGE BASKETBALL

UCLA WON THE NCAA CHAMPIONSHIPS FOR THE 3RD TIME IN 4 YEARS BY BEATING DAYTON, 79–64. UCLA'S CENTER WAS LEW ALCINDOR, WHO LATER CHANGED HIS NAME TO **KAREEM ABDUL JABBAR.**

'67

Oscar night in April 1968 was delayed by the assassination of Dr. Martin Luther King, Jr.

Oscar winners for 1967 films: *In the Heat of the Night* won Best Picture. Also nominated: *Bonnie and Clyde, Doctor Dolittle, The Graduate,* and *Guess Who's Coming to Dinner.* **Mike Nichols** was named Best Director, for *The Graduate.* **Rod Steiger** was Best Actor, for *In the Heat of the Night,* over Warren Beatty, Dustin Hoffman, Paul Newman, and

movies

Spencer Tracy. **Katharine Hepburn** won Best Actress, for *Guess Who's Coming to Dinner,* over Anne Bancroft, Faye Dunaway, Dame Edith Evans, and Audrey Hepburn. **George Kennedy** and **Estelle Parsons** won Best Supporting-Actor Oscars. *Closely Watched Trains* was the Best Foreign Language film, from Czechoslovakia. Best song, *"Talk to the Animals,"* from *Doctor Dolittle,* and best score, **Elmer Bernstein**'s for *Thoroughly Modern Millie.*

18

top-grossing films

1. *The Dirty Dozen* ($18.2 million)
2. *You Only Live Twice* ($16.3 million)
3. *Casino Royale* ($10.2 million)
4. *A Man for All Seasons* ($9.25 million)
5. *Thoroughly Modern Millie* ($8.5 million)
6. *Barefoot in the Park* ($8.25 million)
7. *Georgy Girl* ($7.33 million)
8. *To Sir, With Love* ($7.2 million)
9. *Grand Prix* ($7 million)
10. *Hombre* ($6.5 million)

the american film institute

was founded in 1967, to give government and private support to the industry and to make it more competitive in the worldwide movie scene.

OTHER BIG-EARNING FILMS—*MURDERER'S ROW,* THE REISSUED *GONE WITH THE WIND, EL DORADO, BLOW-UP, WAR WAGON, IN LIKE FLINT,* AND *UP THE DOWN STAIRCASE.*

It was a miserable year for the American auto industry. Sales were in a serious slump. The war and its drain on young male car buyers was one major reason. The buying public was skeptical, too, because of all the

SALES WERE IN A SERIOUS SLUMP.

new safety concerns and equipment in cars. About the only bright spot of the

cars

market were the so-called "sportster" models, of which the Ford Mustang was first, in 1964. Competitors to the Mustang were the Chevy Camaro, Mercury Cougar, and Pontiac Firebird. Vent windows were disappearing. Tapered notchback lines replaced the fastback look on GM's intermediate Chevelle, Tempest, Special, and F-85.

New safety requirements included seat belts for every passenger
seat, padded instrument panels,
fireproof gas tanks, and side cor-
nering lights. There were numer-
ous recalls for safety reasons,
including all 1967 Mustangs for
inspections of steering wheels.

MERCURY
LENGTHENED ITS
COMET INTERMEDI-
ATE AND RENAMED
IT **MONTEGO.**

For many, **twiggy,** the British supermodel with the waif look, epitomized fashion in 1967.

Boots reached new heights. They ranged from ankle-length to thigh-high and hoselike. Pants were designed to be worn everywhere. There were culottes or "city skirts," evening pants that were often like billowing twin skirts, and slim long pinstriped pantsuits.

fashion

YVES ST. LAURENT SHOWED A SAFARI LOOK, WITH SHORT SHORTS.

CHRISTIAN DIOR OF LONDON SHOWED A CHAIN-MAIL TUNIC OVER A BIKINI FOR RESORT WEAR.

Kids' clothing became much more colorful in 1967. Gone were the bows and fussy details. Bold, bright colors and nicely styled clothes were available for children. Stripes were big. Tartans were important for school.

in menswear, a revolution
was taking place. Color was more vivid than it had been for years. Double-breasted styles were favored. Plaids were popu-

lar, as well as cavalry twill, whipcord, and citified tweeds. Men wore turtle-necks under jackets, even for formal wear.

final

factoid

rolling stone magazine
had its first issue in November, published
by then 21-year-old Jann S. Wenner.

ROLLING STONE

MFP

NOVEMBER 9, 1967
VOL. I, NO. 1

OUR PRICE:
TWENTY-FIVE CENTS

Recognize Private Gripeweed? He's actually John Lennon in Richard Lester's new film, How I Won the War. An illustrated special preview of the movie begins on page 16.

Tom Rounds Quits KFRC

Tom Rounds, KFRC Program Director, has resigned. No immediate date has been set for his departure from the station. Rounds quit to assume the direction of Charlatan Productions, an L.A. based film company experimenting in the contemporary pop film.

Rounds spent seven years as Program Director of KPOI in Hawaii before coming to San Francisco in 1966. He successfully effected the tight format which made KFRC the number one station in San Francisco.

Lee Turpin, former program director of KGB in San Diego will replace Tom Rounds at KFRC. Turpin has spent the last year as a consultant in the Drake-Chenault programming service.

The new appointment could mean a tightening up of programming policies. Rounds liberalization of KFRC's play-list may well become more restricted.

THE HIGH COST OF MUSIC AND LOVE: WHERE'S THE MONEY FROM MONTEREY?

BY MICHAEL LYDON

A weekend of "music, love, and flowers" can be done for a song (plus cost) or can be done at a cost (plus song). The Monterey International Pop Festival, a non-profit, charity event, was, despite its own protestations, of the second sort: a damn extravagant three days.

The Festival's net profit at the end of August, the last date of accounting, was $211,451. The costs of the weekend were $290,233. Had it not been for the profit from the sale of television rights to ABC/TV of $288,843, the whole operation would have ended up a neat $77,392 in the red.

The Festival planned to have all the artists while, in Monterey, submit ideas for use of the proceeds.

In the confusion the plan miscarried and the decision on where the profits should go has still not been finally made.

So far only $50,000 has definitely been allocated to anyone: to a unit of the New York City Youth Board which will set up classes for many ghetto children to learn music on guitars donated by Fender. Paul Simon, a Festival governor, will personally over see the program.

Plans to give more money to the Negro College Fund for college scholarships have been discussed; another idea is a sum between ten and twenty thousand for the Monterey Symphony.

However worthy these plans, they are considerably less daring and innovative than the projects mentioned in the spring: the Diggers, pop conferences, and any project which would "tend to further national interest in and knowledge and enjoyment of popular music." The present plans suggest that the Board of Governors, unable or unwilling to make their grandiose schemes reality, will fall back on traditional charity.

The Board of Governors did decide that the money would be given out in a small number of large sums. This has meant, for instance, that the John Edwards Memorial Foundation, a folk music archive at the University of California at Los Angeles, had its small request overlooked.

In ironic fact, what happened at the Festival and its financial affairs looks in many ways like the traditional Charity Ball in hippie drag.

The overhead was high and the net was low. "For every dollar spent, there was a reason," says Derek Taylor, the Festival's PR man and one of its original officers.

Yet many of the Festival's expenses, however reasonable to Taylor, seem out of keeping with its announced spirit. The Festival management, with amateurish good will, lavished generosity on their friends.

• Producer Lou Adler was able to find a spot in the show for his own property, Johnny Rivers; Paul Simon for his friend, English folk singer Beverly; John Phillips for the Group Without A Name and Scott MacKenzie. None of them had the musical

status for an international pop music festival.

It is ironic that the Rivers and the rest appeared "free," but the money it cost the Festival to get them to Monterey and back, feed them, put them up (Beverly
—Continued on Page 7

Airplane high, but no new LP release

Jefferson Airplane has been taking more than a month to record their new album for RCA Victor. In a recording period of five weeks only five sides have been completed. No definite release date has been set.

Their usual recording schedule in Los Angeles begins at 11:00 p.m. in the evening and extends through six or seven in the morning. When they're not in the studio, they stay at a fabulous pink mansion which rents for $5,000 a month. The Beatles stayed at the house on their last American tour.

The house has two swimming pools and a variety of recreational facilities. It's a small small little paradise in the hills above Hollywood. Maybe suntans and guitars don't make it together.

—Continued on Page 7

archive photos: inside front cover, pages 1, 4, 10, 12, 15, 21, 22, 23, inside back cover.

associated press: pages 2, 3, 6, 7, 9, 16.

photofest: pages 8, 11, 19.

original photography:
beth phillips: page 13.

album cover:
courtesy of rustyn birch
page 13

photo research:
alice albert

coordination:
rustyn birch

design:
carol bokuniewicz design
mutsumi hyuga